OUR SOLAR SYSTEM (SUN, MOONS & PLANETS): SECOND GRADE SCIENCE SERIES

SPEEDY
PUBLISHING

Speedy Publishing LLC
40 E. Main St. #1156
Newark, DE 19711
www.speedypublishing.com

Copyright 2015

The Solar System comprises the sun and everything that orbits around it, including planets, moons, asteroids, comets and meteoroids.

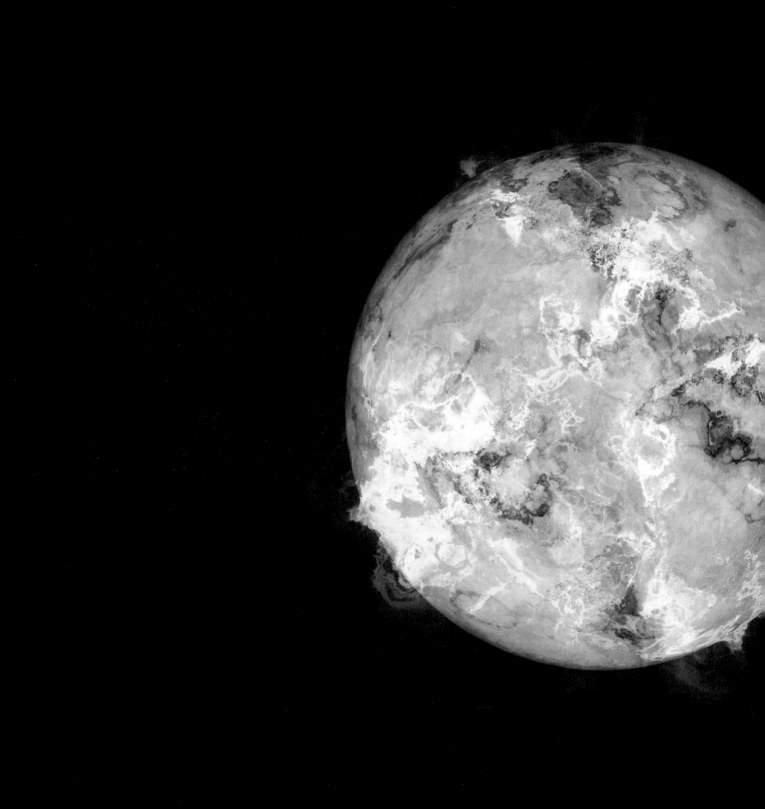

The Sun is the star at the centre of our solar system. The Sun gives life to the Earth. The sun is 150 million km away from the Earth.

Mercury is
the smallest
and closest
to the Sun.
Mercury has
no atmosphere
which means
there is no wind
or weather.

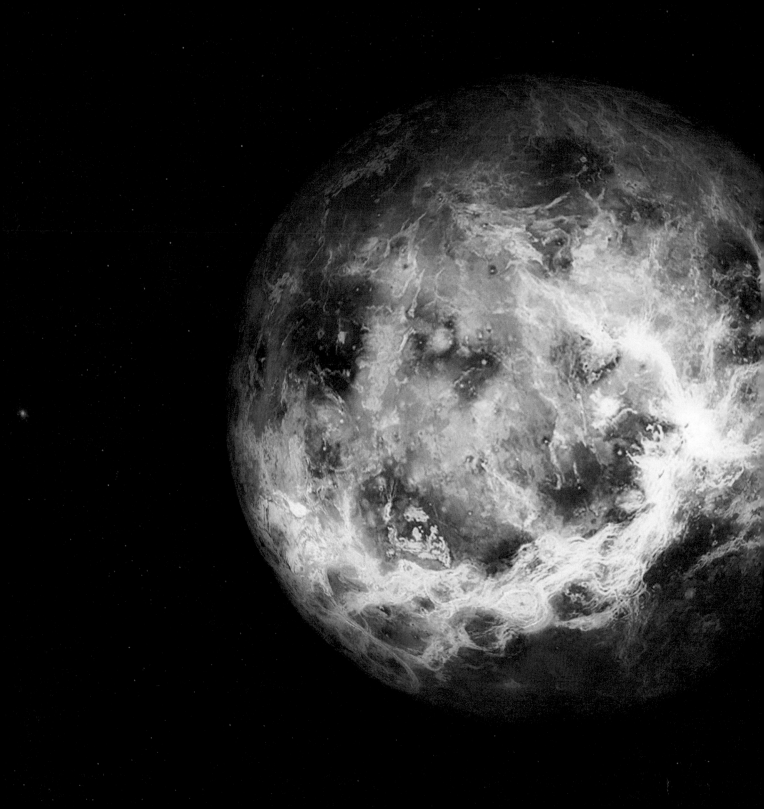

Venus is a terrestrial planet and is sometimes called Earth's sister planet because of their similar size. Venus is sometimes called the morning or evening star.

Earth is the only astronomical object known to accommodate life. Earth is often called the ocean planet. Its surface is 70 percent water.

Mars is often referred to as the Red Planet. Mars has many massive volcanoes.

Jupiter is the largest planet in the Solar System. Jupiter is the stormiest planet in the Solar System.

Saturn is the least dense planet in our Solar System. It is most famous for its beautiful giant rings.

Uranus was the
first planet
discovered
by telescope.
Uranus turns
on its axis once
every 17 hours,
14 minutes.

Neptune is the farthest planet from the Sun. Neptune is the most dense among the giant planets.

Moon is Earth's only natural satellite. It is one of the largest natural satellites in the Solar System.

Titan is the largest moon of Saturn. It is the only moon in the solar system with clouds and a dense, planet-like atmosphere.

Callisto is a moon of the planet Jupiter. Callisto is composed of approximately equal amounts of rock and ices.

Io is the innermost of the four Galilean moons of the planet Jupiter. It has the highest density of all the moons.

Ganymede is the largest moon of Jupiter and in the Solar System. It is the only satellite in the solar system to have a magnetosphere.

Made in the USA
Middletown, DE
08 March 2019